SEYCHELLES TRAVEL GUIDE

Your Essential Travel Companion to Discover Seychelles Hidden Treasure, Natural Beauty and Luxury Islands

CHARLES HUDSON

Table of Content

Seychelles at a Glance

A vacation to the Seychelles archipelago of 115 gorgeous islands is a fantastic way to experience a legendary beauty in the Indian Ocean. It has a land size of 455 square kilometers and a 1.4 square kilometers Exclusive Economic Zone. It is located 1,600 kilometers east of Kenya. The tropical islands are made of either granite or coral. The Mahe Islands, which are largely granitic, are home to the majority of the population. Victoria is the country's lone town and its capital city. It was also the location of the sole port.

The Republic of Seychelles is the official name of the nation. It is a democratic republic, with President James Michel currently in charge. They have a multiparty system and a unicameral legislature.

Seychelles' inhabitants are descended from French colonizers and freed African slaves brought to the nation by the British. The national language is Creole, however English and French are also taught in schools. The current population is above 88,000 people. The majority of people are Roman Catholics, with Anglicans being the largest religious minority.

Seychelles is recognized as a solid economic country, with key businesses including tourism, fishing, copra, vanilla processing, and boat construction. The Seychelles Rupee (SCR) is the national currency.

The weather is pleasant all year. With the nation outside of the typhoon belt, the residents enjoy a lovely tropical marine climate.

Seychelles has a plethora of amazing attractions, from its stunning beaches to its incredible forests, which would enchant any nature lover. There is always an abundance of nice food in the Seychelles. Every tourist will be captivated by their rich and multi-ethnic culture. But the most wonderful aspect of the Seychelles is its nice and welcoming people. It's incredible how they share their paradise.

Brief History of Seychelles

Arab merchants are credited with being the first to visit the Seychelles islands. The first European sighting was made in 1502 by the Portuguese Admiral Vasco de Gama and his crew, who called the islands for themselves, the

Amirantes, or the Admiral's Islands. The British East India Company crew, who had the earliest documented report of the islands, made the first known landfall in the archipelago in 1609. It has become a popular pirate refuge.

The French led a small band of Europeans, Indians, and Africans to the islands in 1756 and administered the islands as part of the developing colony of Mauritius. The French controlled the islands until Napoleon's defeat at Waterloo, when the British took possession through the Treaty of Paris in 1814, changing the French Séchelles name to the Anglicized current name of Seychelles.

The Seychelles gained independence from the British in 1976, becoming a republic while remaining a member of the Commonwealth of Nations. Their first president, James Mancham, had a brief tenure. He was overthrown in 1977 by Prime Minister France-Albert René, who was first sold on the concept of a socialist one-party government but ultimately reinstated a multiparty system alongside several changes. The country had its first multi party system election for the presidency and parliamentary seats in 1993, with President René winning. He campaigned and won again in the presidential elections in 1998 and 2003, but relinquished the presidency to James Alix Michel in June 2004 after 27 years in office. President Michel was elected with a majority of 53.7% of the vote in the 2006 presidential elections.

Seychelles Culture

Seychelles' inhabitants are a colorful mix of British, Chinese, Creole, French, and Indian ancestors. Seychellois people live relatively basic lifestyles in a tourism-conscious country that takes the preservation of the island's natural beauty very seriously. People are very nice because tourism is their main source of income. It is fairly normal to be publicly welcomed to one's home, and guests are expected to offer a gift as a standard courtesy.

The Seychelles is mostly a matriarchal civilization. The mother is usually the dominant member of the household, looking after the children and budgeting family costs. Fathers are legally compelled to support their children. The males have mainly been consigned to providing revenue for the family. In the Seychelles, it is quite usual to encounter single female parents.

Their music reflects a wide range of inspirations. Local musicians reflect the islands' multi-ethnic background by incorporating European contredanse, Polka, mazurka, pan-African genres, French folk and pop, Polynesian, Arcadian, and Indian music. Creole music and dancing abound on the island, frequently accompanied by rhythmic drums and string instruments. The violin and guitar have recently gained appeal among the general public.

Despite having a strong link with the British, French culture has been maintained throughout the islands. Around 70% of the population has French surnames, whereas just 20% have British surnames.

Batik, tablemats, and jewelry pieces fashioned from green snail shells are popular local handicrafts. There is minimal nightlife in the Seychelles; however, there are venues where you may enjoy indigenous music, dancing, and BBQ.

Chapter One
Planning Your Seychelles Trip

Seychelles is a tropical paradise that offers a once-in-a-lifetime experience. Follow our thorough guide to preparing your perfect Seychelles holiday to guarantee your trip is effortless and packed with amazing memories.

Best time to go

When is the best time to go to the Seychelles?

The weather in the Seychelles is affected by trade winds from the northwest and southeast, which generate seaweed growth on numerous beaches. From May to September, the southeast wind blows, whereas the northwest wind blows from November to March.

As a result, the perfect time to visit the Seychelles is between the shoulder months of

April to May and October to November, when trade winds have the least impact. Throughout the year, the weather in the Seychelles maintains about 30 degrees Celsius, with lots of sunlight, refreshing breezes, and tropical showers. These months are perfect for observing animals, diving, and snorkeling.

Seychelles' weather is erratic and complicated, and it rains all year. The peak season in the Seychelles runs from May to September and is ideal for sailing and windsurfing. During these months, the Seychelles receives the most visitors from all around the world and is so overcrowded.

On the other hand, the low tourist season in the Seychelles is typically from November to March. The beaches are typically clogged with seaweed during these months, so if you go during this period, you should select your accommodation carefully. Seychelles also has a bustling tourist season from mid-December to January, which coincides with New Year's and the holiday season across the world.

Visa Requirement

Most nationalities do not require a visa to visit the Seychelles. Visitors are issued entrance visas at the airport after presenting the relevant paperwork for immigration clearance.

The following documents are required: a valid passport on the date of entry and exit from the country (usually with a validity of more than 6 months from the date of entry), a return ticket or a ticket for an onward destination (a return or onward ticket can be purchased upon arrival at the airport), and proof of hotel or housing lodge accommodation (if bookings are made to more than one hotel, a copy for each hotel is required).

In addition to the requisite documentation, travelers must produce adequate finances for the duration of their stay in the Seychelles, equivalent to at least $150 per day, in addition to planned accommodation.

If those conditions are met, a visitor's permission for a stay of up to 30 days will be issued. An extension of up to three months can be acquired after entering the country. Further extensions are permitted for a total of 12 months, with each extension lasting for three months. The first permission is provided free of charge, while future extensions of up to three months are paid at SCR1,000 each.

The Seychelles transit is quite simple. There are no visa requirements for transit. Passengers must have an onward ticket to their final destination. A transit visa must be obtained upon arrival at particular designated ports of entry if a passenger desires to pass through immigration.

How to Get to Seychelles

The only way to get to the island of Seychelles is via flight. Due to several restrictions, mostly for environmental reasons, even entering waterways is not a feasible option.

Getting to Seychelles from India

There are direct flights from Mumbai to the Seychelles. Flights with many stops are available from practically all major cities in the nation, operated by airlines such as Jet Airways, Etihad, Kenya Airways, and Sri Lankan Airlines.

Getting to Seychelles by Flight

Seychelles International Airport is located near the capital Victoria on the island of Mahe and serves as the country's only international gateway. The national carrier, Air Seychelles, provides nonstop flights from Mauritius to Johannesburg, Abu Dhabi, Beijing, Mumbai, and Paris. Taxis to the city center are easily accessible at the airport.

Local transportation in Seychelles
Despite the lack of built transportation infrastructure on the islands, the Seychelles offer a variety of choices for moving around. There are several daily flights between Mahe and Praslin, and the country's Air Seychelles offers multiple weekly or daily flights to other islands.

Zil Air's scenic helicopter ride service is an intriguing way to experience the country's natural splendor. On routes connecting Mahe, Praslin, and La Digue, ferry service is offered with the option of online booking. Taxis and automobile rentals are readily accessible and reasonably priced. Renting a car is an excellent way to see the nation, but you must be at least 21 years old, have a valid driver's license, and drive with caution on the small and steep roads. From dawn to evening, public transportation is accessible on the islands of Mahe and Praslin.

Budgeting and Cost Estimation

A Seychelles vacation does not have to be reserved for wealthy visitors. In this part, we walk you through realistic budgeting tactics and cost estimates to ensure that your trip to this tropical paradise fits within your budget.

Understanding the Seychelles Currency:

- Navigate the Seychellois Rupee (SCR) and learn about its exchange rates to help you manage your budget properly.

- Learn about the benefits of using credit cards and ATMs, as well as how to carry cash for local purchases.

Budget-Friendly Accommodation Options:
- Look at a variety of lodging options, from lavish resorts to budget-friendly guesthouses, to ensure there's something for everyone.
- Learn how to get the greatest bargains, specials, and all-inclusive packages to maximize your lodging budget.

Dining Without Breaking the Bank:
- Explore local markets, street food sellers, and economical cafés to sample Seychellois cuisine without breaking the bank.
- Discover the gastronomic treats that won't break the bank, from fresh seafood to Creole favorites.

Transportation on a Budget:

- Navigate the islands on a budget by learning about the numerous transit alternatives, like public buses, local ferries, and bike rentals.
- Get exclusive tips on cheap transportation options for island hopping excursions and touring other locations.

Activity Money-Saving Strategies:

- Take advantage of low-cost methods to explore Seychelles' natural treasures, such as snorkeling at public beaches and hiking paths.
- Find free or low-cost activities that showcase the beauty of the islands without breaking the bank.

Island-hopping Excursions:

- Learn how to arrange budget-friendly island-hopping excursions, including advice on finding low-cost lodging and transportation.

- Visit lesser-known islands that offer unique experiences at a lower cost.

Cultural Experiences on a Budget:

- Immerse yourself in Seychelles culture without breaking the bank by participating in local events, festivals, and cultural activities.
- Learn how to truly connect with the Seychellois way of life, from touring markets to attending community activities.

Seychelles becomes an accessible paradise for tourists of all socioeconomic backgrounds by learning the art of budgeting and cost estimation. This section equips you to make educated decisions, ensuring that your Seychelles vacation is not only memorable but also cost-effective. Prepare to be wowed by the Seychelles' beauty without breaking the bank.

Packing Essentials

Strategic packing becomes your passport to a flawless and joyful vacation as you prepare to step foot on the enchanting islands of the Seychelles. We present detailed tips on important items that will enhance your trip and ensure you are well-prepared for all aspects of your Seychellois vacation in this area.

Lightweight Clothing for the Tropics

Navigate the Seychelles' tropical environment with a well-curated wardrobe of lightweight, breathable apparel. Pack comfortable clothing for beach trips, island explorations, and star-gazing dinners.

Swimwear and Snorkeling Gear

Pack your favorite swimwear and snorkeling gear to dive into the crystalline seas of the Seychelles with confidence. Remember to bring sunscreen, a rash guard, and a waterproof phone cover to capture those aquatic moments.

Comfortable Footwear

The Seychelles need comfortable and adaptable footwear, from sandy beaches to lush mountain slopes. Include beach sandals, robust hiking shoes for nature paths, and casual alternatives for exploring local shops and sites.

Sun Protection Essentials

Protect yourself from the tropical sun by bringing high SPF sunscreen, a wide-brimmed hat, sunglasses, and after-sun care products to keep your skin rejuvenated.

Lightweight Rain Gear

Although the Seychelles have a tropical climate, rain showers are a normal part of the experience. Pack a small, lightweight rain jacket or poncho to keep you dry without taking up too much luggage room.

Insect Repellent and First Aid Kit

Prepare for outdoor outings by packing bug repellent to keep mosquitoes at bay. Pack a basic first-aid kit with items like sticky bandages, antiseptic wipes, and any personal prescriptions you might need.

Power Adapters and Electronics

Pack the appropriate power adapters for the Seychelles to ensure you stay connected and record every moment. Remember to bring your camera, smartphone, and other electrical gadgets, as well as a portable charger, for longer expeditions.

Snacks and a Reusable Water Bottle

Bring a reusable water bottle to stay hydrated in the tropical atmosphere. Pack snacks for on-the-go energy, especially if you intend to tour nature areas or go island hopping.

Lightweight Daypack

Pack a lightweight daypack to simplify your adventures. This flexible item is ideal for taking necessities for day outings, whether hiking, exploring local markets, or relaxing at the beach.

Travel documents and Essentials

Keep your travel papers safe, including your passport, airline tickets, and hotel bookings. To protect your necessities from unexpected tropical showers, consider purchasing a waterproof document organizer.

By prioritizing these packing requirements, you will not only be well-prepared for the many adventures that Seychelles has to offer, but you will also guarantee that your journey is pleasant, easy and full of amazing memories. Prepare your bag and get ready for a once-in-a-lifetime Seychellois trip.

Chapter Two
Planning Your Itinerary

A trip to the heavenly archipelago of the Seychelles promises turquoise waters, verdant landscapes, and cultural charm. To guarantee that your Seychellois vacation runs well, detailed itinerary planning is essential. This chapter will walk you through the process of designing a custom itinerary that captures the spirit of each island, reveals cultural riches, and immerses you in the Seychelles' natural beauties.

Choosing Your Islands: Seychelles has 115 islands, each with its own distinct personality. Begin by choosing the islands that correspond to your trip choices. Popular destinations include Mahé, Praslin, and La Digue, which offer an ideal combination of beaches, culture, and natural beauty. For a more private encounter, continue your exploration with excursions to Silhouette, Bird, or Félicité.

Duration of Stay: Determine how long you will spend in the Seychelles. A week provides a well-rounded experience, while two weeks allow for further in-depth exploration. Consider your preferred trip speed, whether it's a leisurely walk around each location or an immersion dive into individual islands.

Accommodation Options: Seychelles accommodates a wide range of accommodation choices. There are luxury resorts, boutique hotels, guesthouses, and self-catering villas to choose from. Choose from beachfront villas with direct access to the Indian Ocean and hillside getaways with panoramic views of beautiful surroundings.

Transportation Logistics: Plan your inter-island transit. Connectivity is provided by domestic aircraft, ferries, and speedboats. Book inter-island flights ahead of time for convenience, and make sure ferry timetables coincide with your itinerary.

Cultural Exploration in Victoria: Set aside time in Mahé to explore the capital city of Victoria. The colorful Sir Selwyn Selwyn-Clarke Market, the distinctive Clock Tower, and cultural sites such as the National Museum and the Natural History Museum are well worth a visit.

Natural Excursions: Include nature trips on your agenda. On Praslin, see the Vallée de Mai, a UNESCO World Heritage Site, and on Mahé, explore the trails of Morne Seychellois National Park. Choose guided nature hikes to learn about the Seychelles' flora and animals.

Beach Bliss and Water Activities: Make time for beach exploration and water activities. Famous beaches include Anse Lazio on Praslin and Anse Source d'Argent on La Digue. Explore the Seychelles' varied marine life via snorkeling, diving, and sailing.

Island-Hopping Adventures: Include island-hopping excursions in your schedule. Explore the granite boulders of La Digue, the coral atolls of Alphonse and Desroches, or the peculiar vegetation of Silhouette. Each island offers another element to your Seychellois story.

Culinary Delights: Try Seychellois cuisine in local restaurants and fine dining venues. Taste Creole delicacies like fish curry and meals with coconut. For a real experience of the Seychelles, don't miss out on the bustling street food scene.

Wellness and Relaxation: Take advantage of wellness retreats and relaxation. The Seychelles have spa retreats and yoga experiences set against magnificent natural scenery. Relax with revitalizing treatments and discover peace in the serene settings of the islands.

Local Festivals & Events: Check the calendar for upcoming festivals and events in your area. Visit the Festival Kreol or the Carnaval International de Victoria to see the Seychelles' lively cultural events.

Artisanal Explorations: Make time for artisanal exploration. Visit marketplaces and stores to interact with Seychellois artisans. Participate in workshops to make your own Seychellois-inspired souvenirs, which will add a personal touch to your vacation.

Flexible Downtime: Make room in your agenda for flexible relaxation. The allure of the Seychelles is found in unexpected discoveries and serendipity. Allow for impromptu beach picnics, hikes, and long-lasting sunsets.

Weather Considerations: When planning your trip, keep the weather in mind. The northwest monsoon (dry season) lasts from November to March, while the southeast monsoon (wet season) lasts from May to September. Make appropriate plans for outside activities.

Local Interactions: Interact with the locals to have a better understanding of their culture. Participate in community activities, traditional dances, and chats to experience the warmth of Seychellois hospitality.

Documenting Memories: Finally, make time to capture memories. The breathtaking scenery and rich culture of the Seychelles provide several chances for photography, journaling, and creating a visual record of your Seychellois experience.

As you meticulously prepare your Seychellois schedule, keep in mind that every day is an opportunity to immerse yourself in the islands' enchantment. Create an itinerary that reflects your travel goals, enabling the Seychelles to reveal their beauties at your own pace. Your Seychellois experience is more than simply a journey; it's a one-of-a-kind tapestry of discovery ready to be weaved.

Chapter Three
Unique Accommodation Experiences

Seychelles entices with the promise of more than simply a holiday, but of an unequaled escape into luxury and comfort. This chapter unravels the fabric of one-of-a-kind lodging experiences that raise your stay to the level of remarkable moments.

Overwater Bungalows and Luxury Resorts

Seychelles is a true paradise: a stretch of tropical islands surrounded by a turquoise sea, with wild wildlife, breathtaking scenery, and some of the world's top luxury hotels and resorts. Still not convinced? Begin planning your next holiday with the comprehensive list of the Seychelles' Top 7 Luxury Resorts.

Four Seasons Resort, Mahe, Seychelles

The Four Seasons Resort Seychelles elevates the bar for tropical beach resort luxury by being perfectly outfitted, tastefully built, and marked by a superb holiday vibe. It's ideal for couples as well as families with children.

One thing to admire is the natural setting. This home is nestled among lush tropical foliage and constructed on high hills that flow down to the beach, which happens to be one of the most gorgeous beaches we've ever seen.

This location will provide you with several opportunities to shoot that envy-inducing Instagram shot.

Anantara Maia Seychelles Villas

An extravagant refuge that exceeds tropical luxury sits high above a stunning beach of opalescent sand lapped by the azure ocean, surrounded by swaying palms. This specialist spa resort is nestled in a wonderfully lovely environment, providing the ideal respite from the busy pace of contemporary life. Bill Bensley designed the guest villas, which are high-spec, low-impact constructions that allow optimum solitude while preserving the stunning natural surroundings.

We like it because of the villa style and layout. Each features its own pool and a separate pavilion with a large couch.

North Island, Seychelles

There are just a handful of island resorts like this one in the world. North Island is stunning and secluded, engulfing visitors in a carefree and casual attitude. Its design mixes natural beauty with pure enjoyment, as well as a totally personalized experience with no dress rules. It's for people looking for their own untouched, magnificent dream island.

We adore it for: the natural beauty of the island, the large villas, the great nature (turtles!), and the absolute seclusion, as well as the carefree, bare-foot relaxed attitude with no dress requirement.

Four Seasons Resort, Desroches Island

Desroches Island, which is remote and secluded yet only 35 minutes (by tiny plane) from Mahé, is well located to deliver a "luxury castaway" experience courtesy of Four Seasons. This is due in large part to the fourteen kilometers of white beaches that encircle the island, as well as the untamed wildlife that exists inside its core. On Desroches Island, the Four Seasons Resort Seychelles includes 40 beach suites with private pools and 11 private home villas. Every villa has a living room and a bedroom that opens onto expansive terraces with a 19-square-meter pool overlooking gorgeous private gardens. Guests may live out their desert-island imaginations by participating in unique events such as sunset-watching from a lighthouse.

We like it because of the beauty of the residences. Four Seasons designed ideal suites for couples seeking peace and leisure.

Banyan Tree, Mahe Island, Seychelles

The spectacular Banyan Tree Seychelles combines sophisticated elegance and outstanding service in a traditional, quasi-colonial hotel surrounded by tropical foliage, commanding a breathtaking view of the Indian Ocean, and facing one of the most gorgeous beaches. The Banyan Tree Seychelles is an outstanding alternative for couples and honeymooners, with a world-class spa, quiet pool villas, and a fantastic location.

We like it because: the resort is positioned above one of Seychelles' nicest beaches, if not the best we've seen. It's large and spectacular, bordered by granite rocks, with smooth white sand and shade offered by overhanging palm trees.

Constance Lemuria Praslin, Seychelles

The Constance Lemuria Resort lies on Praslin, Seychelles' second-largest island, and is home to the Vallée de Mai Nature Reserve (home to the rare Coco de Mer trees). The resort's guest accommodations are placed along two gorgeous beaches and are no more than fifteen meters

from the water. Constance Lemuria offers two
three-level swimming pools, access to three
lovely   sandy   beaches,   and   its   own
championship eighteen-hole golf course.

The Presidential Suite is the resort's premium
lodging choice. It is nestled among granite

rocks on the southern side of the property and offers solitude and elegance.

Denis Private Island, Denis Island

Denis Private Island is a self-contained tropical getaway that immerses guests in nature. This modest private paradise is geared toward families with children and is proud of its conservationist efforts. It is covered by a lush forest and is home to several local bird species and big tortoises.

The resort's twenty-five beautiful cottages each have their own individual personality and are located apart from one another. Their isolation makes them feel like they're on their own desolate island. All have immediate beach access and décor that resembles upscale beach villas.

It embodies barefoot luxury in its simplest form. This island is a place for you to disconnect from the contemporary world and reconnect with what truly matters.

Boutique Hotels and Eco-Friendly Stays

Villa Sancta Maria

Villa Sancta Maria is located in Mahe, about an 8-minute walk from Anse à la Mouche Beach and about 1.8 kilometers from Anse Louis Beach. This apartment has a patio and free private parking. The on-site personnel can arrange for a shuttle service.

The vacation house has two bedrooms, a fully equipped kitchen with an oven and a toaster, and a kettle. The patio, which also offers outdoor furniture, provides guests with views of the sea. The lodging is non-smoking.

Guests at this apartment may go on local walking excursions or enjoy the grounds.

Villa Sancta Maria is 13 miles from the Seychelles National Botanical Gardens, while Victoria Clock Tower is 13 miles away. The nearest airport is Seychelles International Airport, which is 6.8 miles away.

Eden Island Apartment 70A14

Eden Island Apartment 70A14, located within a 2-minute walk from Anse Tec-Tec Beach and

500 yards from Anse Bernik Beach, offers Eden Island lodgings with an open-air bath, a casino, and a bar. This seaside apartment has a balcony, a pool table, and complimentary WiFi. The property features an infinity pool with a pool bar, spa services, and a 24-hour front desk.

The large apartment has two bedrooms, a living area, a satellite flat-screen TV, an equipped kitchen, and two bathrooms with a walk-in shower and a bidet. The patio, which also offers outdoor furniture, provides guests with views of the mountain. The room offers a private entrance and soundproofing for increased privacy.

Guests may dine at the family-friendly restaurant on-site, which is open for supper, lunch, brunch, and beverages.

The 5-star property has table tennis and tennis courts. Snorkeling and walking excursions are offered nearby, and there is also a vehicle rental facility and a private beach area on-site.

Petit Amour Villa, Seychelles

Petit Amour Villa, Seychelles, is located in Victoria, a 10-minute walk from Northolme Beach, and features an outdoor swimming pool, free private parking, a garden, and a communal lounge. The 5-star hotel's rooms all have mountain views and complimentary WiFi. The restaurant serves American and Cajun Creole cuisine, and the bar serves drinks.

Each room at the hotel has air conditioning, a wardrobe, a terrace with a view of the sea, a private bathroom, a flat-screen TV, bed linen, and towels. Certain rooms at Petit Amour Villa in Seychelles have pool views, and all rooms have a balcony. Rooms at the accommodation have a sitting space.

Breakfast is served every day, and selections include à la carte, continental, and full English/Irish.

Petit Amour Villa in the Seychelles is a 13-minute walk from Sunset Beach, while

Tusculum Beach is 1.1 kilometers away. Seychelles International Airport is 11 miles away from the hotel.

Kempinski Seychelles Resort

Kempinski Seychelles is located at the privileged south end of Mahé, near the famed Baie Lazare, and provides exquisite rooms with a balcony or terrace. This resort has an outdoor pool and spa services.

The rooms at Kempinski Seychelles Resort are large and nicely designed, with modern oak furnishings. All air-conditioned rooms include a balcony or a private patio, a satellite TV, iPod docking stations, tea/coffee making facilities, and a mini-bar.

Café Lazare serves a breakfast buffet as well as themed buffet dinners. L'Indochine serves a variety of classic cuisines. Windsong Bar serves cocktails and appetizers, while Planter's Lounge and Bar features live music every evening.

The Olympic-length pool at the resort is great for relaxing, and there is a new gym close to the pool for fitness aficionados. Guests may participate in activities such as snorkeling and kayaking. There are six treatment rooms available at the spa.

Chateau Elysium

Chateau Elysium, located in Beau Vallon on Mahe Island, has a garden and views of Beau Vallon Beach. The facility has both rooms and villas. There is free WiFi and private parking available.

The main villa suites have a seating room, patio or balcony, and access to a TV lounge. There are also individual villas on the site, each with a living room, private kitchen, plunge pool, balcony, patio, and gazebo.

You may participate in a variety of sports, including snorkeling and diving. The resort is 8.1 miles from Seychelles International Airport.

Villa Blanc

Villa Blanc is located on Mahe Island's Beau Vallon and overlooks the Indian Ocean. This luxurious property is set in a private neighborhood, 98 feet from Beau Vallon Beach. It has a sun deck with its own outdoor pool.

The villa is furnished in modern white tones and has two bedrooms, one with a king-size bed and the other with a double bed. It has a living room with a flat-screen cable TV as well as a fully equipped kitchen. There is free WiFi in all places.

Guests enjoy immediate beach access, and a water shower is available at the private beach gate.

Diverse activities, such as sailing, fishing, and snorkeling, are available in the vicinity.

Ocean View Villa, Beauvallon villas

Ocean View Villa - Beauvallon Villas is a beachfront home with a view of the sea and private beach access. It has a garden with a sun patio.

The property features three bedrooms and three bathrooms. Towels and bed linen are provided.

There is a living room with a sofa and a flat-screen television.

Meals may be prepared in the fully equipped kitchen and served in the dining room or outside.

Car rental is accessible on-site, and the surrounding region offers a variety of activities such as diving, sailing, and fishing. Snorkeling is common in the region.

Local Guesthouses and Cultural Immersion

Rowsvilla Guest House

Rowsvilla Guest House, located 656 steps from the white sand Beau Vallon Beach, offers self-catering apartments with a patio and free onsite parking.

The air-conditioned flats come with a kitchenette that includes a refrigerator and an oven. There is also a lounge with a flat-screen TV and a private bathroom in the bedroom.

The Victoria Market is only 2.5 miles away, while the Botanical Garden is only 3.1 miles away. Rowsvilla Guest House is located 8.1 miles from the Seychelles International Airport and 11 miles from the Seychelles Golf Club.

Forest Lodge

Forest Lodge is near Bel Ombre, about a 15-minute walk from Beau Vallon Beach. There is a garden, BBQ facilities, and a restaurant on the premises. There is free WiFi available.

Each air-conditioned room at Forest Lodge has a flat-screen TV with satellite channels and a telephone with free local calls. There is also a balcony and a full kitchenette with a microwave and a refrigerator. A shower is also provided in the private bathroom. Views of the mountains and gardens are available.

Forest Lodge can help you with car rentals and airport transportation.

Panorama Guesthouse and NEW Apartments Beau Vallon

This guest house is within a minute's walk from the world's most famous beach. Panorama Guest House & Apartments, located directly on Beau Vallon Beach, provides new self-catering apartments as well as classic guest rooms with beach views.

The new apartment has an open-plan living room with a well-equipped kitchen, a dining area, and a TV lounge. Modern, minimalist décor, air conditioning, and a balcony or patio There are two shower bathrooms.

Traditional guest rooms on the ground level with views of the beach and direct access to the garden. Each room features a fan and air conditioning, a safe, and a bathroom with a shower.

There is a patio with outdoor seating and free private parking at the original Creole House. There are sun loungers in the garden, as well as a snorkeling spot 50 meters to the right and a bus stop immediately next door.

On the beach, there is a diving facility as well as restaurants and bars. A 10-minute drive away is Victoria, with its History Museum, Market, and Inter Island ferry.

Orchid Sunset Guest House

The Orchid Sunset Guest House is located on Mahe Island in Anse La Mouche. There is free WiFi available. Each room at this hotel has air conditioning. Ironing facilities and a fan are available as extras.

A garden, BBQ facilities, and a patio are available at Orchid Sunset Guest House. Other amenities available at the site include free parking.

The Seychelles International Airport is 15 kilometers away.

Rising Sun Guest House

Sun Rising Guest House in La Digue offers contemporary accommodation with a garden and a patio. With bike rental, the resort is located 500 meters from Anse La Reunion's sandy beach.

Each air-conditioned room has a patio, a refrigerator, and an electric kettle. The private bathroom has a shower.

On-site dining options include Creole cuisine.

Sun Rising Guesthouse is 1 km from the Inter Island Ferry and 1.5 km from the La Digue Boatyard.

SeaBreeze Villa

SeaBreeze Villa is nestled on the hillside of Anse Royale, only a short walk from the beach. It has a garden and offers free WiFi.

All rooms at the guest home have a balcony with a view of the sea. Each room has a private bathroom and cable TV.

The resort provides a continental breakfast.

Guests will have access to the living and dining rooms, as well as the verandas on the ground and first levels, and kitchen access may be offered upon request.

Villa Kayola Self-catering

Villa Kayola - Self Catering is located on Mahe Island, 15 minutes' walk from the beach at Anse aux Pins. On-site private parking is free.

Each apartment has a sitting area. Some units feature a patio or balcony with views of the sea or mountains. There is also a dining room and a kitchenette with a microwave, a toaster, a fridge, and a burner, as well as a kettle. Each unit has its own bathroom with a shower and toilet. Towels and bed linen are available. All of the rooms include free WiFi and air conditioning.

Seychelles International Airport is 6 kilometers from the unit.

Chapter Four
Getting Around

Seychelles, a beautiful Indian Ocean island nation, is a popular tourist destination noted for its beautiful beaches, crystal-clear seas, and teeming marine life. To fully appreciate what this archipelago has to offer, you must be aware of the transit alternatives available on the islands.

Public Transportation

Seychelles' public transportation system is small, with only a few buses running on the three main islands of Mahé, Praslin, and La Digue. Local buses are inexpensive and convenient; however, they might be congested during peak hours. Buses frequently operate from early morning until late at night, and the tickets are inexpensive, making them an excellent choice for budget tourists.

Taxis in Seychelles

Taxis are frequently accessible throughout the Seychelles and are a wonderful way to tour the islands at your leisure. Taxis use a metered fare system, with rates varying based on time of day and distance traveled. To prevent being ripped off, it is best to negotiate the price before embarking on your journey.

Car Rental in Seychelles

Another simple and convenient means of transportation in the Seychelles is automobile rental. Having a car allows you to explore the islands at your own speed and visit out-of-the-way locations. Several automobile rental businesses provide a variety of vehicles, ranging from little budget cars to bigger SUVs. However, while driving, have your driver's license and other essential paperwork with you.

Bicycle Rentals in Seychelles

Many people believe that riding is the best way to see the islands, and renting a bicycle is a great alternative for them. Cycling is a fantastic way to explore the Seychelles' hidden jewels and go off the main path. Most hotels and guesthouses on the islands offer bike rentals.

Boat Ferry Services in Seychelles

Boat ferries are an important means of transportation in the Seychelles, linking the main islands with the offshore islands. Ferries go from Mahe to Praslin, La Digue, and other smaller islands. These boat services offer a calm and leisurely method to travel across the Seychelles and enjoy its natural beauty.

Seychelles has a variety of transportation options to assist you in touring the islands. Whether you prefer public transportation, renting a vehicle or bike, or using water ferry services, the island country has something for everyone. Seychelles transportation is manageable, safe, and convenient, guaranteeing that you have a pleasant vacation in this paradise.

Chapter Five
Things to Do in Seychelles

To make the most of your Seychelles vacation, immerse yourself in a variety of activities that will leave you with memories that last a lifetime.

Snorkeling in Seychelles

In the Seychelles, snorkeling is one of the best water sports. Observing the marine life of the Seychelles is a delightful experience due to its pristine blue sea. Also, the coral and marine life of the Seychelles are highly developed due to the protection of the surrounding waters. You can go snorkeling in the Seychelles right off the beach or while on a trip to a snorkeling location.

In the Seychelles, snorkeling offers the chance to witness some incredible marine species, such as corals, manta rays, turtles, butterflyfish, surgeonfish, pufferfish, parrotfish, and angelfish. Bringing your own mask, snorkel, and flippers is recommended. On the other hand, Seychelles dive centers and resorts also rent out snorkeling gear.

The months of April and November offer the highest underwater visibility, making them the ideal times to go snorkeling in the Seychelles. The best time to snorkel alongside hawksbill turtles is from August to February; however, if you want to snorkel among sharks, you should travel between October and January. Avoid May to September for the best access to the beach and underwater sports since seaweeds cover the entire shoreline.

Diving in Seychelles

In the Seychelles, diving is one of the most well-liked activities. You may be certain of the greatest scuba diving experience in the Seychelles thanks to the more than 70 dive sites spread over the area and the year-round favorable temperature for diving. The best underwater scenery is created by coral reefs, rocks, caverns, and sunken ships, and visibility can reach up to thirty meters. The Seychelles have dive sites ranging in depth from 8 meters at the shallowest to 30 meters at the deepest. You can travel to pristine places on private boats. Professional courses are also available to ensure your safety.

Top Diving Centers in Seychelles

- Seychelles Diving Cruises Ltd.
- Big Blue Divers
- Blue Sea Divers Seychelles
- Octopus Diving Center
- Blue Safari Seychelles Diving
- Hawksbill Dive Center
- Seychelles Underwater Center

- Whitetips Divers

According to reports, the diving seasons in the Seychelles are April, May, October, and November. At this time of day, the water's temperature is about 29 degrees Celsius, and visibility is above 30 meters.

Hiking in Seychelles

One of the best tourist activities in the Seychelles is hiking, which is made breathtakingly gorgeous by the rocky landscape and endemic diversity. Every trail has clear markings. The granite islands of Mahe, La Digue, and Praslin feature breathtakingly beautiful mountainous landscapes.

The top hiking routes in the Seychelles are as follows:

Seychelles, known for its stunning beaches and crystal-clear waters, also offers hiking enthusiasts a chance to explore its lush landscapes and scenic viewpoints. Here are 12 of the best hiking trails in the Seychelles, each offering a unique perspective on the archipelago's natural beauty:

Copolia Trail (Mahé)

A moderately challenging trail leads to the summit of Copolia Hill, providing panoramic views of Mahé and the neighboring islands.

Morne Blanc Trail (Mahé)

Ascend to the highest point on Mahé, Morne Blanc, for breathtaking views of the island, its coastline, and the Indian Ocean.

Anse Major Trail (Mahé)

A coastal hike starts from Bel Ombre to Anse Major, passing through granite cliffs and lush vegetation and offering secluded beach views.

Glacis Trois Frères Trail (Mahé)

Navigate this trail to reach the Trois Frères peaks, where sweeping views of Beau Vallon and Silhouette Island await.

Nid d'Aigle Trail (Mahé)

A challenging trek to the "Eagle's Nest," offering unparalleled vistas of Mahé's west coast and surrounding islands

Mont Signal Trail (Praslin)

Hike through the Vallee de Mai Nature Reserve to Mont Signal, enjoying a scenic journey through the UNESCO World Heritage Site.

Fond Ferdinand Nature Reserve (Praslin)

Explore the reserve's trails, including the Coco de Mer and Glacis Noire trails, for encounters with unique flora and fauna.

Anse Lazio to Anse Georgette (Praslin)

A coastal trail links two of Praslin's most famous beaches, providing stunning sea views along the way.

Mare Aux Cochons Trail (La Digue)

Venture through tropical forests and ascend to the island's highest point, offering panoramic views of La Digue and its surrounding islands.

Grand Anse to Anse Cocos (La Digue)

A coastal hike leads to the pristine Anse Cocos, passing by Grand Anse and Petite Anse for diverse beach experiences.

Le Viole Forest Hike (Silhouette)

Explore Silhouette Island's lush forests on this trail, encountering unique flora and fauna along the way.

Mount Dauban Trail (Fregate)

Ascend Mount Dauban on Fregate Island for breathtaking views of the surrounding Indian Ocean and neighboring islands.

These hiking trails in the Seychelles promise not only physical adventure but also a chance to connect with the archipelago's unique biodiversity and pristine landscapes. Whether you seek panoramic viewpoints, secluded beaches, or encounters with rare wildlife, the

Seychelles' trails have something to offer every nature enthusiast.

Sunbathing in Seychelles

The best places to obtain a tan are the beaches at Beau Vallon, Anse Lazio, Anse Georgette, and Anse Source D'Argent. Enjoy the abundance of nature by lying in the sand, paddling in the shallows, and taking a romantic, daring stroll along the beaches. In case you're in the mood for some excitement, the beaches feature activities like jet skiing, water skiing, snorkeling, and scuba diving.

Zip Lining in Seychelles

To secure your place for this popular activity, book a spot in advance. You get to explore the vegetation, wildlife, and canopy of the forest. Choose one of your eight available zip line ranges, then take off over your favorite scenery! This is ideal for family vacations because it's safe for both adults and kids.

Copolia Trail in Seychelles

The best trail in the nation for those who love to hike and trek is Mahe Island's Copolia Trail! The trail climbs to breathtaking granite peaks. Views of the islands, beaches, and the enigmatic, exotic blue Indian Ocean are available to you from above. For a good time, consider leaving early in the morning.

Helicopter Tour in Seychelles

Taking a helicopter trip over the immaculate islands is one of the best ways to take in the breathtaking beauty of the Seychelles. You can see the gorgeous combination of turquoise and white with lots of flora. There is nothing like the nighttime view from the helicopter. Hotels and private agents in the Seychelles offer the tours.

Kayaking in Seychelles

Kayaking in the Seychelles is a tropical paradise for many people. The dazzling blue sea and gentle current make it ideal for paddling and experiencing the ocean at its most enthralling. The crystal clear water provides several possibilities for observing marine species in their native habitat.

Hiring a kayak and paddling around Anse Volbert and adjacent Chauve Souris Island is a nice pastime for anyone with time. This may be done at your own leisure, taking in everything this place has to offer in a unique and unusual way.

Kayaking is a flexible activity that may be enjoyed by individuals of all ages. However, basic paddling abilities are required. It's the best way to get from one island to the next and visit isolated locations off the beaten path.

In the Seychelles, a tandem bicycle (two persons) is great for families and couples looking for once-in-a-lifetime experiences. The path from Round Island to Moyenne Island is popular for kayaking since the water is quiet and clean. Kayak adventures are organized by highly skilled specialists and are a must-try sport on Seychelles Island.

Fishing and Deep-Sea Excursions

The Seychelles, a sanctuary of blue seas and diverse marine life, invites visitors to explore the depths of the Indian Ocean through exciting fishing and deep-sea adventures. We throw a line into the rich seas around the islands in this section. Join us on this extraordinary adventure where the excitement of the catch meets the peace of the open sea.

The Pursuit of Trophy Fish: Explore the world of sportfishing as the Seychelles provide some of the best possibilities to catch prize fish. The deep-sea seas teem with opportunities for fishermen looking for the ultimate catch, whether it's the adrenaline-pumping challenge of catching a marlin or the sheer power of a sailfish.

Fishing Charters and Guides: Navigate the boundless ocean with experienced fishing charters and qualified guides who know the ins and outs of the Seychelles' maritime riches. These experts reveal secret fishing areas and offer an immersive experience for both novice and seasoned fishermen, from Mahé to the distant atolls.

Trolling in Pristine Waters: Discover the art of trolling as sleek vessels cut through the waves, lines trailing in expectation. Mahé,

Praslin, and La Digue provide unique trolling experiences, letting you enjoy the excitement of the pursuit while surrounded by the Seychelles' stunning landscape.

Bottom Fishing Adventures: Dive into the realm of bottom fishing and discover the wealth of the ocean floor. Pursue snappers, groupers, and other reef-dwelling species, generating exciting moments against the backdrop of vivid coral reefs and granite structures.

Big Game Fishing Festivals: Join in the fun at the Seychelles' big game fishing festivals, where fishermen from all over the globe gather to compete and appreciate the richness of marine life. These competitions not only exhibit the competitive spirit but also create brotherhood among fishermen against the gorgeous background of the islands.

Island-Hopping Fishing Excursion: Enjoy the excitement of fishing while exploring the Seychelles' hidden jewels on island-hopping fishing trips. Hop between Mahé, Praslin, La Digue, and the outlying islands, casting your line in a variety of marine settings and finding each destination's own appeal.

Fly Fishing on the Seychelles Flats: Discover the skill of fly fishing on the small flats that surround the islands, where bonefish and the rare permit await. The Seychelles are a well-known location for fly fishermen looking for the thrill of sight fishing against the backdrop of gorgeous blue seas.

Night Fishing Adventure: Night fishing trips beneath the Seychelles' star-studded skies will transform your fishing experience. Cast your line into the darkness, where the waterways come alive with nocturnal species and the potential for unexpected encounters, for a new type of pleasure.

Sustainable Fishing Practice: In the Seychelles, embrace the idea of sustainable fishing, where a commitment to conservation assures the preservation of marine habitats. Participate in eco-friendly charters and projects that promote appropriate fishing techniques, enabling you to experience the thrill of the catch while contributing to the ocean's long-term health.

Culinary Adventures with Your Catch: Bring the excitement of your fishing trip to the dinner table by participating in culinary adventures with your catch. Work with local cooks to turn your freshly caught fish into wonderful Creole meals, giving you a firsthand taste of the Seychelles' marine riches.

Deep Sea Exploration and Marine Life Encounters: Aside from fishing, deep-sea expeditions provide opportunities to interact with the Seychelles' varied marine life. Join skilled guides for snorkeling lessons to see the beauty of coral reefs, turtles, and colorful fish, offering a comprehensive marine journey for all lovers.

Customized Fishing Packages: Customize your fishing experience with packages tailored to your needs, whether you're a lone fisherman, a family looking for adventure, or a group of friends looking for a group marine trip. Seychelles fishing charters and operators ensure that your trip is completely personalized.

The fishing and deep-sea adventures in the Seychelles promise an oceanic symphony of adventure, relaxation, and marine marvels, from the hunt of prize fish to sustainable practices and gourmet delights. Cast your line into the vast ocean and let the rhythm of the waves lead you through this enthralling maritime adventure.

Chapter Six

The Best of Seychelles

Seychelles, a refuge for the discerning visitor, beckons with a tapestry of experiences that exemplify the very essence of luxury and calm. "The Best of Seychelles" is a selected trip through the most unique features of this island paradise.

Top Rated Seychelles Attraction Centers

The Seychelles are a haven of unmatched beauty where blue waters meet verdant landscapes, nestled in the center of the Indian Ocean. Seychelles, which enchants tourists with its distinct fusion of pure environment, lively culture, and opulent retreats, is home to several highly regarded attractions that guarantee life-changing experiences. Here, we present a fascinating mosaic of the must-see locations in the Seychelles:

Vallée de Mai Nature Reserve (Praslin)

Do you need a vacation from the sea, sand, and sun? Make your way to Vallée de Mai National Park's shaded, calm corners. For those who enjoy the outdoors, this is among the greatest spots to visit in the Seychelles.

Situated on the island of Praslin, this verdant park, recognized as a UNESCO World Heritage Site, safeguards an ancient forest that is home to at least 4,000 unique specimens of the Seychelles-only big coco de mer fruit palm.

Numerous lizard species and uncommon birds, like the black parrot, which is the national bird of the Seychelles, fruit pigeons, and Seychelles bulbul, call the valley home.

It is strongly advised that you hire a guide in order to gain more knowledge about flora and fauna. Keep in mind that park admission is not free.

Anse Lazio (Praslin)

One of the most stunning beaches in the Seychelles is Anse Lazio (Chevalier Bay), which is located on the north side of Praslin Island. The beach is accessible by a hillside trek, but we assure you that the effort is worthwhile.

This lengthy stretch of silky golden sand blends with crystal-clear seas in lovely colors of blue, surrounded by rounded granite rocks. Beachgoers may find areas of shade to relax under the shade of tamarika trees and coconut palms, and there are eateries at both ends of the beach for those who get hungry.

Early morning or late afternoon, when most tour buses have departed, is the ideal time to explore Anse Lazio.

Anse Source d'Argent (La Digue)

Anse Source d'Argent is a photographer's dream come true, known for its distinctive granite rock formations, pristine seas, and famous coconut palm-fringed beach. A classic beauty that appears on a lot of postcards.

Morne Seychellois National Park (Mahé)

Morne Seychellois National Park is a haven for hikers and nature enthusiasts. Over 20 percent of Mahé is covered by this, the largest national park in the Seychelles.

Enclosed inside its verdant boundaries is the mountain range known by the name of Morne Seychellois, its highest peak, rising to a height of 905 meters and providing a commanding view of Victoria's capital.

In addition to a variety of indigenous palm species, such as pandanus, pitcher plants, ferns, and sunbirds, the wildlife includes numerous noteworthy bird species, such as the Seychelles scops-owl, bulbul, and sunbird.

Hikers may access the Baie Ternay and Port Launay Marine Parks by strolling west across the park. The remote beach at Anse Major and the village of Bel Ombre are located to the northwest.

Ste Anne Marine National Park

Ste Anne National Marine Park was established in 1973 and is the first national park in the Indian Ocean. It is located 15 to 20 minutes by boat off the coast of Mahé, close to Victoria, and comprises six islands.

Discover the great range of marine life in the park's coral reefs via snorkeling, scuba diving, and glass-bottom boat tours. Most of the islands within the reserve may be explored on day trips from Mahé. A number of the islands allow overnight stays as well.

Hawksbill turtles use Sainte Anne Island as a major breeding place. Despite the presence of crocodiles and mangroves, the island hosted the first French colony in the Seychelles in 1770.

Seychelles Natural History Museum (Victoria, Mahé)

The Seychelles Natural History Museum is a brilliant representation of the rich natural and cultural legacy of the country. This museum offers an interactive investigation of the remarkable biodiversity of the island by weaving a compelling story about the flora, fauna, geology, and anthropology of the Seychelles. This cultural institution, which is conveniently placed close to Victoria's main post office, serves as an important stop along the path through the fascinating history of the Seychelles.

The museum's extensive exhibitions skillfully encompass seven essential aspects of the Seychelles' natural inheritance, which are exhibited through an enthralling blend of displays and lifelike dioramas. However, this museum offers more than simply a flat depiction of the natural history of the nation.

It serves as an engaging and instructive forum that provokes important conversations on important environmental issues. Its goal is to raise awareness of the dangers that the Seychelles face and motivate residents and tourists to take action for conservation.

Aldabra Atoll

Aldabra is the world's biggest elevated coral atoll and a UNESCO World Heritage Site. Through four channels, the center lagoon fills and empties twice a day, revealing mushroom-shaped pinnacles known as champignons.

Tiger sharks and manta rays frequent the shallows, and the atoll is home to hundreds of species, including the Indian Ocean's sole flightless bird, the white-throated rail. Lesser and bigger frigate birds, red-footed boobies, dimorphic egrets (found only here and in Madagascar), Aldabra sacred ibis, greater flamingos, and the Malagasy kestrel are also on display.

There are 200,000 giant tortoises on Aldabra, which is five times the amount found on the Galapagos Islands.

It is difficult to visit this secluded island since you can only get there by chartering a private boat, and you must first receive permission from the Seychelles Islands Foundation.

Aldabra AtollAldabra Atoll

The Copolia Trail is a 1.4-kilometer-long nature trail on the island of Mahé, close outside Victoria. This moderately challenging track has a gentle climb--don't worry, it's not too strenuous.

The finest view is from the peak, which is 488 meters above sea level. A well-hiked trail will reward you with panoramic views of Victoria and the stunning turquoise ocean. In terms of hiking, plan on spending around an hour there and back, with more time if you want to relax at the summit.

Wooden boardwalks guide travelers through the lush rainforest, while moss-covered rocks offer a magical touch. Wear comfy shoes and keep your phone fully charged. You'll want it to take a ton of pictures.

Bird Island

Bird Island, formerly known as Îles aux Vaches due to the presence of dugongs (sea cows) in the vicinity, is home to a migratory sooty tern population that grows to one million, five hundred birds during the nesting season, from May to October. Birders and photographers can access the nests by climbing to elevated viewing platforms.

On the island, there are also fairy and noddy terns, cardinals, ground doves, mynas, crested terns, and plovers. There are also enormous land tortoises on the island, and big-game fishing is popular on the adjoining Seychelles Bank.

The only place to stay on the island is Bird Island, Seychelles, a simple self-catering eco-lodge. The island is accessible via a 30-minute flight from Mahé.

Victoria, Mahé

The little capital of the Seychelles, on the island of Mahé, is the country's only harbor and was named Port Victoria after the British queen following her coronation.

The main attractions can be explored in a single day. The Seychelles National Botanical Gardens are a popular tourist destination. The gardens, which were established about a century ago, include 15 acres and include native and exotic species, as well as flying foxes, gigantic tortoises, and an orchid garden.

In recent years, contemporary concrete and glass buildings have grown up across the city, with the few remaining colonial structures clustered around Freedom Square. The most prominent historical feature is the clock tower. It was built in 1903 and was designed after

Little Ben, a smaller counterpart of Big Ben in London.

St. Paul's Cathedral, which overlooks the plaza, was erected on the site of the Seychelles' first church, which was devastated by a severe hurricane in 1862.

Shoppers go to Sir Selwyn Clarke Market, where locals sell fish, fresh fruits and vegetables, and gifts ranging from ship models to pearl jewelry.

The Natural History Museum, which also houses a few historical relics, provides an overview of the Seychelles' flora and animals.

Aride Island Nature Reserve Day Trip

Aride Island Nature Reserve, the northernmost of the Granitic Seychelles, is home to 18 species of seabirds, including frigate birds, red-tailed tropicbirds, and the world's biggest colonies of lesser noddy and roseate terns.

Nature enthusiasts will discover the largest density of lizards on the planet, as well as numerous rare floral species. Wright's gardenia, also known as bois citron, is only found on this island.

Most Praslin Island hotels can arrange day tours to Aride; however, keep in mind that the island is frequently closed to guests from May to September owing to severe surf. Helicopter tours are also available.

Curieuse Island Day Trip

Curieuse Island, once known as Île Rogue because of its russet-toned dirt, is now home to a breeding facility for giant tortoises, who walk freely throughout the sandy coves.

The majority of the island is covered with takamaka and casuarina trees, which shade the white-sand beaches, but Curieuse is also noted for another botanical distinction: it is the only spot in the world, other than Praslin, where the coco de mer palm grows naturally.

The island was also originally a leper colony, and you may visit the remnants of the leprosarium on the south coast, as well as the restored doctor's home.

Boat cruises from Praslin Island take you to Curieuse Island.

Recommendation on Best Beaches

The person who created the phrase "paradise" must have visited the Seychelles. This idyllic archipelago of around 115 islands off the east coast of Africa in the Indian Ocean is a region of unrivaled beauty, having several of the world's greatest beaches.

The sand on these magnificent beaches is so fine that it heals weary feet, in addition to its brilliant blue waves, many sea turtles, and an underwater environment teeming with colorful life. With a gorgeous backdrop of lush forests, massive rocks, and grassy hills, you'll get a sense of the area's beauty.

With so many untouched, picture-perfect beaches in the Seychelles, it might be difficult to select which to visit for a romantic couple's holiday or honeymoon and which to visit for a family-friendly trip you'll remember for years.

Our selection of the top beaches in the Seychelles will help you narrow down your search for paradise.

West Beach, Bird Island

West Beach is a pearly sand sanctuary that tenderly caresses tired feet. This Bird Island refuge offers a stunning perspective packed with unequaled hues of orange, red, pink, and purple, making it one of the greatest beaches in the Seychelles to watch a sunset.

What a secluded beach! This beach is located on the northernmost island in the Seychelles archipelago, 96 kilometers from Mahé. It's so peaceful and lonely that turtles feel courageous enough to explore and lay their eggs there.

Bird Island, which is protected on both its east and west sides by a barrier reef, is an ideal location for getting up close and personal with underwater snorkeling. Head to adjacent Hirondelle Beach.

The island's robust bird life is very well recognized, hence the name. Bird Island is home to about one million Sooty Terns.

Anse Cocos, La Digue

One of the nicest things to do on La Digue Island is to visit Anse Cocos Beach. You'll understand why after you see its postcard-worthy splendor. Massive granite boulders dot the sparkling white beach, perfectly offset by water so blue you'd assume it was colored by Crayola.

A journey to Anse Cocos, like most worthwhile endeavors, takes some effort. That entails a 30-minute walk from the adjacent Grand Anse beach. Its remote location, on the other hand, means you won't have to fight crowds, which is a nice treat for anyone searching for a little romance and seclusion on their beach vacation.

Explore the tidal pools along the foot of the boulders for unusual animals; paddle about in the quiet, shallow water at the bay's edge; or simply relax on the smooth sand while staring out at a view that will melt any tension. When you're feeling warm, head to the surf or find shade under a palm tree.

Petite Anse, La Digue

This curved cove on the southeast coast of La Digue is frequently named among the best 10 beaches in the Seychelles, and it is overlooked by the Four Seasons Resort. They've erected a swing for an envious photo opportunity. Non-guests must park at the gates and walk down, but a nice member of staff will generally wave you down and transport you back up the steep slope in a resort cart.

Anse Georgette, Praslin

The phrase "pristine" is overused when describing beaches, yet Anse Georgette deserves it. The grounds of the five-star Constance Lemuria have risen around this modest sand grin, but it is still a public beach.

Despite demands to provide parking, a café, and sun loungers, the hotel has battled to maintain its raw natural beauty, making it one of the Seychelles' few unspoiled beaches. There is no coral, and the currents can be strong owing to the sheer drop-off.

Anse Forbans, Mahe

Anse Forbans is the place to go if you want to unwind. This beach is perfect for families, romantics, and people wishing to relax due to its shallow, peaceful, and vivid blue sea. While swimming and sunbathing are the most popular activities, many people also enjoy snorkeling and fishing in the tranquil water.

Anse Forbans, located on Mahé's southeast coast, has also attracted beach hotels such as the four-star Doubletree by Hilton Seychelles - Allamanda Resort and Spa. That's not always a negative thing, because it means you'll be able to locate restaurants, lodging, and water activities nearby.

Anse Forbans Chalets

Despite its closeness to hotels, this beach is never overcrowded. In fact, you may frequently have it practically entirely to yourself.

Anse La Passe, Silhouette Island

Anse La Passe is a magnificent beach that hugs the western shore of Silhouette Island (approximately 19 kilometers north of Mahé). It is part of the exquisite, all-villa Hilton Seychelles Labriz Resort & Spa.

Silhouette Island, the third biggest in the Seychelles archipelago, is car-free and home to just approximately 100 people. If you're searching for a peaceful beach holiday, this is the place to go.

The warm ocean that surrounds this island is a protected marine park that boasts an undisturbed paradise rich with marine life. Anse La Passe's gorgeous length of beach is lapped by crystal-clear, quiet sea. A healthy coral reef is about 200 meters offshore, making this an ideal location for families.

When the tide is out, all you have to do is wade in ankle deep to see an amazing spectacle.

Everything from lionfish to stingrays to eels may be seen without the use of a snorkel and mask. Spiky sea urchins lurk amid the coral, so tread carefully.

Other enjoyable activities, such as sailing, bicycling, and fishing, are accessible so close to the resort, as is wonderful food from a variety of restaurants.

Anse Intention, Mahé

Anse Intendance, like most of the stunning Seychelles beaches, is renowned for its iridescent turquoise ocean and surrounding lush tropical jungle. The only thing lacking is a coral reef, but this is really a benefit—no reef equals superb surfing.

While Anse Intendance is normally gorgeous and tranquil, it is not the finest beach for families on the island. The strong waves and currents that thrill surfers make swimming challenging for both the younger generation and other, less competent swimmers, particularly from June to September.

This untamed beach on Mahé's southwestern coast is home to the elite Banyan Tree Seychelles, a romantic beach resort where vacation visitors are treated to individual pool villas in a magical setting.

It is, however, positioned well back, making it an inconspicuous addition to the beach. Furthermore, the hotel's handy position is advantageous for sunbathers searching for a bite to eat, as there are no stores or other concessions on this isolated beach.

Anse Louis, Mahé

Anse Louis, like most of the greatest Seychelles beaches, has been occupied by a vacation resort.

The Anantara Maia Seychelles' unassuming homes dot the verdant mountainside, each with its own infinity pool. That's a plus for other travelers: because hotel guests are too busy enjoying the finer things in life, you won't have to contend with crowds at this wonderful, pristine beach.

Anse Louis is located on Mahé's west coast and is placed in a tiny, protected harbor, which adds to its exclusivity. It has 500 meters of coastline and is located between two more beautiful beaches, Anse à la Mouche and Anse Boileau. This is an excellent beach for couples seeking romance.

The big, granite rocks that have made this place renowned may be found near the north end of the beach, as well as a tropical jungle demanding to be explored. The south end is better for resting and swimming, while the north side has bigger surf-worthy waves. From June to September, seaweed is likely to wash up on the beach.

West and Honeymoon Beaches, North Island

The North Island is home to five of the Seychelles' greatest beaches. They're also among the most exclusive, as they can only be enjoyed by guests of the exclusive and ultra-private North Island, a Luxury Collection Resort.

With only 11 ultra luxurious villas, visitors can expect a tranquil, five-star experience complete with top facilities, great service, drool-worthy meals, and, of course, access to some of the world's best beaches. This is where celebrities such as George and Amal Clooney, as well as royals Will and Kate, honeymooned.

West Beach has the nicest sand and the most breathtaking sunsets. It is the longest beach on the North Island, stretching along the majority of the west coast. The water is quiet and clean here, making it ideal for snorkeling and scuba diving. There is lots of shade on the land, making it easy to remain there all day.

Honeymoon Beach is located on the top of a tiny bay and is easily accessible by a modest hike up Bernica Hill. This picturesque beach is popular with couples and is excellent for a romantic picnic, which the hotel will provide, so you don't have to bring anything.

Please keep in mind that the route to the beach is rugged, so wear appropriate footwear.

Anse Major, Mahé

Anse Major is a hidden gem on Mahé's northwest coast that can only be reached by foot or boat.

Because there are no roads leading to this hidden paradise, you'll have to park and trek in, which can take anywhere from 30 to 60 minutes. The reward: breathtaking views of the coast from atop a granite cliff, as well as a quiet setting that's hard to surpass. You're not a walker? There are also water taxis available.

When your feet touch the soft, untouched sand, you'll understand that your journey was worthwhile. The famous blue sea of the area hugs the coast, which is surrounded by lush green vegetation. The tranquil ocean makes this one of the island's safest spots to swim, making it ideal for a relaxing swim.

Insider's Tip: Go to the beach early in the morning (before 9) to escape the harsh heat, as the walk provides minimal shelter. Also, because there are no services on the beach, bring lots of water, food, and anything else you might need.

Chapter Seven
Seychelles Cuisine and Dining

In the center of the Indian Ocean, where blue oceans meet pristine coasts, Seychelles appears not only as a feast for the eyes but also as a culinary haven. Set off on a culinary adventure that will reveal the rich tapestry of Seychellois cuisine—a delectable blend of tastes fashioned by African, Asian, and European influences. Let's explore the world of Seychelles Cuisine and Dining, where each dish celebrates the islands' rich past.

A Taste of Seychelles' Foods

French, British, Spanish, Indian, African, and Chinese cuisines all had an impact on Seychelles cuisine. Fish is a popular staple due to its position in the Indian Ocean. Rice, shrimp, shellfish, shark, breadfruit, mango, and curries are among the popular Seychelles dishes. In the Seychelles, popular alcoholic beverages include palm wine, rum, and indigenous beer (Seybrew and Eku).

So, here are some of the Seychelles' most popular meals that you should absolutely try:

Grilled Fish

For those who enjoy eating fish, you'll be surprised at the diversity of fish dishes available in this nation, which range from smoked, steamed, baked, and coated in banana leaves. Grilled fish is a must-try food here, and it's made by cooking fish filled with garlic, chili, and ginger over hot BBQ coals. Barracuda is a common fish cooked in this manner. Add a cold drink, a stunning view of the ocean, and some fantastic people, and you've got yourself the perfect evening.

Coconut Curry

Another must-try meal in the Seychelles is the ever-popular Coconut curry, which is typically served with rice. This creamy curry is made by frying onions, ginger, garlic, and a variety of masala spices until the kitchen fills with the wonderful scent of the meal.

To finish this classic Creole recipe, freshly produced coconut cream is combined with curry leaves and a touch of saffron. The curry is mildly hot, and the blend of spices used to prepare it distinguishes it from other curries. As a result, this is a meal that you should absolutely eat while visiting these islands.

Bat Curry

If you want to try something unusual, one of the most popular delicacies among Seychelles' huge selection of unique food is bat curry. While some tourists find the thought of eating bat curry, which is made from the flesh sliced from the wings of fruit bats, repulsive, locals love it. Anse Soleil Restaurant and Marie Antoinette Restaurant are two of Seychelles' most famous restaurants, featuring classic Creole cuisine such as Bat curry.

Kari Bernik

Kari Bernik, or limpet curry, is a Seychelles delicacy that is rarely consumed since it requires a lot of effort to prepare. This meal is produced by cooking limpets, which are comparable to barnacles, with coconut milk, eggplant, and a local masala/curry powder. To appreciate this cuisine, one must first develop the taste.

Cassava Cake

Cassava pudding, or cake, which originated in the Philippines, is a popular gelatinous dish in the Seychelles. It's more like a jiggly cake than a pudding, and it's made with cassava, a starchy root vegetable, milk, sugar, vanilla extract, and other ingredients. It's finished with finely shredded coconut, which adds a little crispy texture.

Shark Chutney

While chutney is commonly served as a side dish with various cuisines in India, Seychellois consider shark chutney to be much more than a lowly side dish. This one-of-a-kind but tasty chutney is made by cooking and mashing shark meat and combining it with lime, turmeric, fried onion, and bilimbi (a Seychelles native fruit). It is available at practically every Creole restaurant in the country and may be enjoyed alongside your main course.

Breadfruit

Your journey to the Seychelles would be incomplete if you did not sample breadfruit, one of the key traditional ingredients of these islands. This fruit, which smells like freshly made bread, is a vital ingredient in a variety of recipes offered here, whether grilled, baked, barbecued, boiled, steamed, microwaved, or fried.

Breadfruit chips are a popular snack item on these islands, and you may often find travelers snacking on these salty fried chips while visiting. Breadfruit is frequently blended with coconut milk and served as a dessert dish called 'Ladob'. Locals and tourists alike frequently request second helpings of this wonderful delicacy.

Bouyon Bred Fish Soup

Bouyon bred, a particularly nutritious Seychelles cuisine dish, is a transparent broth cooked with fresh moringa leaves and fried fish. This meal, derived from the French term "bouillon" or "bouillir," which means to boil, can be eaten alone or with rice. Bouyon bread is also consumed to aid in recovery after a cold or flu since it is high in nutrients.

Salad Palmis

Salad Palmis, also known as "Millionaire's Salad" in the Seychelles, is a delicacy made mostly from the heart of a palm tree. It consists of a silky, milky white center surrounded by delicate flesh. The salad also includes chopped green tomatoes, avocados, green mangoes, coconut, red bell peppers, coriander, and mint in addition to the primary component. The ingredients are then topped with a ginger and lime sweet and sour dressing.

Ladob

Ladob is a traditional item in Seychelles cuisine, either as a savory side dish or as a dessert. Ladob is made sweet by cooking ripe plantains and sweet potatoes (or cassava, corossol, and breadfruit) with coconut milk, nutmeg, vanilla pods, and sugar. It is made savory with salted fish cooked with coconut milk, nutmeg, cassava/breadfruit/plantain, and salt. This meal can be served either hot or chilled.

Salted Fish

Salted fish, also known as Pawson salé in the Seychelles, is a popular dish created by salting and sun-drying freshly caught fish. This is done to preserve the fish and give it a unique flavor.

This salted fish may subsequently be used to make a variety of cuisines, including chatinis (chutneys), rougail (tomato-onion sauce), fried rice, and fish curries. It can also be served fried with rice and papaya chutney.

Lentils

The humble lentil is an often ignored meal, yet it is an important side component of a classic Seychelles curry feast. Red lentils are a common staple in the Seychelles, where they are offered as a side dish with a variety of cuisines. These are frequently cooked for an extended period of time with garlic, onion, and ginger, resulting in a yellow mixture.

This may not appear to be particularly appetizing, but it is quite good. If you have the option, definitely include some in your meal.

Dining in Seychelles

Here is a list of the top 20 restaurants in the Seychelles, each with a full description of what makes them special:

La Scala (Mahé)

La Scala, located atop the Northolme Resort, provides a classy dining experience with amazing views of the Indian Ocean. This restaurant specializes in Italian and international cuisine, with dishes made with precision and flair. It is known for its exquisite ambiance and great service.

Boathouse Bar and Grill (Mahé)

The Boathouse Bar and Grill on Eden Island is a seaside treasure known for its relaxing environment and wonderful fish. Guests may relish a selection of grilled treats while taking in the magnificent views of the ocean, making it the ideal location for a casual yet unforgettable dining experience.

Marie Antoinette (Mahé)

Marie Antoinette, located in a gorgeous colonial mansion, is a gastronomic refuge for visitors looking for a genuine taste of Creole food on Mahé. The friendly environment of the restaurant and classic cuisine combined with local tastes and spices offer a remarkable dining experience that represents the Seychelles' cultural richness.

Boardwalk Bar and Grill (Praslin)

Boardwalk Bar and Grill, located in Constance, Lémuria, offers a magnificent seaside location as well as a diversified menu that focuses on seafood and foreign cuisine. The contemporary design, excellent service, and sound of the waves combine to create a magnificent ambiance for a romantic or celebratory lunch.

Café des Arts (Praslin)

Enjoy the visual and gastronomic mix at Café des Arts on Praslin. This one-of-a-kind restaurant mixes Seychellois and foreign tastes while displaying local art in a lively gallery environment. Guests may sample inventive cuisine while admiring the work of local artists.

The Old School Multi-Cuisine Restaurant (Digue)

The Old School on La Digue, housed in a colonial-style structure, serves a fusion of Seychellois, Indian, and international food in a comfortable environment. The vintage charm of the restaurant, along with its excellent cuisine, creates a lovely experience that takes diners to a bygone period.

Chez Jules (La Digue)

Chez Jules on La Digue is a must-visit for genuine Creole eating. Set in a tropical garden, the restaurant provides a range of Seychellois cuisine that highlights the islands' unique culinary traditions. The relaxed atmosphere adds to the appeal of this renowned cafe.

Portofino (Mahé)

Portofino, perched on Eden Island, is synonymous with sophisticated Italian restaurants and a lovely waterfront vista. This restaurant succeeds in creating traditional Italian meals with fresh, high-quality ingredients while also transporting customers to the Mediterranean's coasts.

Les Rochers Restaurant (Mahé)

Les Rochers Restaurant, tucked away in the thick vegetation of Mahé, is known for its seafood specialties and calm setting. Guests may taste the aromas of the sea while being surrounded by nature, making it a great location for a romantic supper or a peaceful vacation.

Bazar Labrin (Mahé)

Bazar Labrin, located in Beau Vallon, provides a colorful, market-style eating experience. This open-air restaurant embodies the vivid essence of Seychelles' culture and cuisine, with live music and a range of Creole delicacies, making it a popular choice for both residents and visitors.

The Maharajas (Mahé)

The Maharajas of Mahé are a gastronomic treasure for those who enjoy Indian food. This restaurant offers customers a gourmet trip through the rich tapestry of Indian culinary traditions, with a cuisine offering authentic flavors and a refined environment.

The Pirates Arms (Mahé)

The Pirates Arms, located in the center of Victoria, is a historic tavern and restaurant famed for its colonial charm and wide menu. The pub-style environment, along with foreign food, makes it popular among residents and tourists looking for a relaxed yet unique eating experience.

Ristorante Da Pasquale (Mahé)

Ristorante Da Pasquale, located in Anse Royale, is well-known for its authentic Italian cuisine. The restaurant gives a taste of Italy against the backdrop of the Seychelles' tropical splendor, with a concentration on using fresh, local foods.

The Anchor Café (La Digue)

The Anchor Café, which overlooks the port in La Passe, is a beautiful destination for seafood lovers. This beachside café captures the spirit of island living with a gorgeous location and a cuisine emphasizing freshly caught goodies.

Coco Rouge (Mahé)

Coco Rouge, located in Victoria, is a wonderful café noted for its handmade coffee, scrumptious pastries, and welcoming ambiance. The café's dedication to excellent products and a welcoming atmosphere make it a favorite among both residents and visitors.

Fisherman's Wharf (Mahé)

Fisherman's Wharf on Eden Island has a seafood-centric meal in a colorful environment overlooking the marina. The restaurant offers a gourmet trip through the Seychelles' seaside delights with a diversified menu that includes Creole favorites.

Cap Lazare (Mahé)

Cap Lazare, located on Takamaka Bay, blends outstanding seafood meals with a beautiful beachside environment. Guests may enjoy exquisite cuisine while listening to the sounds of the ocean, making it a popular venue for special occasions.

Le Repaire Boutique Hotel & Restaurant (La Digue)

Le Repaire on La Digue is a boutique hotel restaurant with a comfortable atmosphere and a broad menu comprising Creole, Italian, and international cuisine. The restaurant offers a pleasant yet polished dining experience, with a focus on using local ingredients.

Kannel Restaurant (Mahé)

Kannel, located at the Raffles Seychelles, impresses with its beachfront position and a menu that combines Seychellois and foreign flavors. The exquisite location and culinary brilliance of the restaurant make it a favorite of both visitors and discriminating diners.

Les Dauphins Heureux (Praslin)

Les Dauphins Heureux is a private seaside restaurant surrounded by beautiful hills on Praslin's southern shore. The restaurant provides a calm respite for those wanting a private and clean dining experience, with a tranquil setting and a menu using fresh, local foods.

The above Seychelles restaurants demonstrate the gastronomic diversity of the archipelago, ranging from beachside seafood delights to ancient pubs and lovely cafés. Each location offers customers the opportunity to experience Seychelles delicacies in various surroundings that reflect the spirit of the islands' natural beauty and cultural depth.

Nightlife in Seychelles

The Seychelles is a popular destination for great nights out. It is a center of entertainment for its guests, with various clubs, pubs, discos, and casinos. As the sun sets, life in the Seychelles takes on a whole new meaning. The clubs warmly welcome you and promise you a memorable night. Behind the showers of beauty is the island nation's fun-filled nightlife. People who live or vacation here like spending their nights outside. We give you a few possibilities where you may stake your nights and never be sorry.

Tequila Boom

Tequila Boom has managed to keep its reputation as the most lively location to spend a night on the archipelago since it first opened its doors to guests. The club is air-conditioned and big, and it even features VIP booths. Go-Go dancers would frequently set the floor on fire. From traditional Seychellois music to current hip-hop, you'll find it all at this one-stop shop, which is also one of the greatest spots to enjoy Seychelles nightlife.

Oxygen

Oxygen is a must-visit nightclub in Praslin, offering a lively nightlife. Locals and tourists flock to it as soon as the sun goes down for its fantastic music and mind-boggling throng. No matter how amazing the place is, it has higher entry requirements. You must be properly attired. There are no sleeveless t-shirts, shorts, or flip-flops permitted.

Gran Kaz Casino

"Explore the Magic of Where Winners Play." According to the casino's motto, Gran Kaz has set the benchmark for providing the greatest gaming experience in the Seychelles. The availability of both table and slot games entices you to spend an exciting evening with cards and poker. The casino offers both classic reel machines and high-tech slot machines. The vibrant and colorful surroundings make visiting here a visual delight.

Casino Des Iles

This casino is the most visited on one of the most beautiful islands in the world, Praslin. There is a restaurant, ten table and poker games, and fifty gambling machines under its eaves. You may play blackjack, poker, and roulette here. It also has backgammon, which is a special favorite of the owner, a former Dutch champion.

Pallagames Slots Bar

Pallagames operates three locations in Mauritius and one in Praslin, each with over 300 slot machines and 26 table games. 1 Zero Roulette, Poker, Black Jack, Dice Games, and Van Lak are among the games available. You may take turns while sipping cocktails or other refreshing drinks. The live music here is totally melodic, so you'll have a nice time.

Amusement Centre

The Amusement Center, the most popular casino, has 200 loose slot machines. It has a solid reputation for dishing out the most substantial jackpots. Their exclusive responsibility is to their consumers. The atmosphere is distinctive, and while the space is modest, it fits nicely within your budget. The atmosphere is ideal for socializing and gambling. It is one of the Seychelles' oldest casinos.

Barrel Nightclub

Barrel Night Club is Victoria's brightest star, known for its reggae music. It offers pool tables outside the club doors for lounging and a beautiful subterranean dancefloor where people dance to hip-hop, local music, and Creole.

The Night Club is ideal for hosting events on a budget. It provides you with a place to be yourself and a place to breathe in the life around you. It is definitely one of the trendiest venues in the Seychelles to enjoy the nightlife. The best way to describe Barrel Nightclub is as a roof where you can bond with the locals.

Night Markets: Would You Like to Shop at Night?

A starry sky and hands full of shopping bags! What a fantastic combination! This is available at the Beau Vallon night market. This night market, located on one of Mahe's most beautiful beaches, will make you go crazy. There are about 20-30 booths where you may shop and dine. Fresh food, spices, fish, art and cultural goods, and handicrafts are also available.

Although there are more vendors for street food, there are also choices for shopping for other items. You should not miss any of them since they provide delectable local food. Furthermore, Seychelles never misses an opportunity to amuse you, so you will find some of the sellers singing and even dancing for you. The market is held every Wednesday and last Saturday of the month, beginning at 4:00 p.m.

Watching Movies - Go, find Bollywood in Seychelles

If you enjoy watching movies, you'll be glad to hear that Seychelles, despite its distant position, boasts a theater. Deepam Cinema in Victoria is our recommendation. This is the only cinema on the island, and it is open until 12:00 a.m.

As a result, you may get some food and relax while watching Bollywood, Telugu, Hollywood, and French films. The hall seats 247 people and features a powerful sound system. As a result, if viewing movies is your thing, pay a visit.

Ah, dinner on the beach! Sounds promising

Nothing beats dining in a setting when the beach air whispers in your ears and the moon pours its wonderful light over you. Most of us only consider this in our imaginative minds. But wait! You may make your fantasy a reality while in the Seychelles. Because of its wonderful position, Seychelles boasts several oceanfront restaurants where you may light candles and dine by the beach. To mention a few examples.

Chapter Eight
Exploring Seychellois Culture

The Seychelles is an archipelago of 115 islands in the Indian Ocean off the east coast of Africa. Seychelles, which borders tourist attractions such as Mauritius and the Maldives, is a peaceful region with numerous deserted islands that is excellent for a relaxing holiday. Because the majority of Seychellois are immigrants, the culture has been heavily influenced by the blending of many races--African, European, French, and Indian. Even more intriguing is the fact that the culture is matriarchal, with women wielding authority at home.

So, let's have a look at the Seychelles' diverse and dynamic culture.

Seychelles Festivals

The Creole Festival

If you wish to see the merging of cultures from several ethnic groups in one area at the same time, the Creole Festival is not to be missed. Every year in October, this week-long event provides a getaway from the mundane. Dive into the sea of cultures and discover different cuisines, beverages, music, and dancing, all with a multi-racial twist. The event takes place on the islands of Praslin, La Digue, and Mahe.

The Creole Festival pays homage to the vibrant culture, customs, traditions, and practices of the Creole way of life.

Seychelles Ocean Festival

The Seychelles Ocean Celebration is an annual underwater celebration held in December. Photographic contests, school events, diving, and snorkeling are all part of the festival.

It is largely observed to remind Seychellois of their abundant underwater reserves and the need to safeguard and maintain them. What's more, you can show off your underwater photography abilities while winning some truly great prizes.

The Feast of Mary's Assumption

This is a local celebration held on the island of La Digue. Praslin and Mahe devotees also attend the celebrations. It is a religiously significant celebration conducted in the Church of La Digue (Christianity is the major religion of the Seychelles).

People pray to the Virgin, Mother Mary, and ask for her blessings.

Seychelles Cuisine

The food of the Seychelles reflects the flavors of France, Africa, India, and Europe. As an island country, the basic diet is a variety of fish and shellfish dishes, as well as coconut, mangoes, and breadfruit. Other mouth-watering foods to try are ladob and shark curry. Ladob is a creamy sauce composed of sweet potato, plantains, coconut milk, nutmeg, and vanilla that is eaten as a dessert.

You can't go wrong with the savory form of ladob, which is made with salt, a little spice, plantains, and cassava. Shark curry, on the other hand, is made with mashed, skinned shark with bilimbi juice, lime, salt, and fragrant spices. If you visit Seychelles, you must try the mouthwatering bat curry (Civet de chauve souris), cassava pudding, fruit bat, and Satini Rekin, which are all inspired by flavors from France, Africa, and India.

If you like wine, you should taste the Seychelles' specialties: palm wine calou (or kalou), bakka rum, Seybrew, and Eku. The cuisine of the Seychelles is a unique blend of flavors from many areas that you just must sample.

Seychelles Traditional Dance

Do groove to African rhythms the Seychellois way: moutia, a traditional Seychelles dance. Moutia, with its profound origins in the history of African enslavement, is the focal point of all Seychelles festivals and festivities. Moutia is just swinging your hips to and fro to the beats of African music in a fun way.

The Sega dance is another ancient but unusual Seychelles dancing form. Women in wide frill skirts swing their waists in the most enthralling way, and you can't help but join them. To top it all off, Kanmtole is a ballet influenced by

European culture. You don't want to miss any of these unusual and distinctive dance routines, especially if you're a party animal!

Seychelles Music

If you're in the Seychelles, your heart will rush to the rhythms of zez, bom (Brazilian berimbau), polka, taarab, soukos, French folk and pop, and Sega. Seychelles music, which dates back over 200 years, makes considerable use of percussion instruments. The most popular is the tangy Moutya, whose songs may often be heard at bazaars along the shore.

Seychelles music has its own form of European contredanse called Kontredans, as well as reggae dubbed Seggae and Mouggae (mingled with Sega and Moutya melodies). Zouk is a new genre in the Seychelles that combines traditional music with modern, fast-paced sounds.

Seychelles Arts and Crafts

Seychelles has few original works of art and craft. However, if you wish to uncover some historical and traditional Seychelles handmade products, the Seychelles handmade village is a must-see. The Craft Village serves as a reminder of the Seychelles' diverse cultural history.

The town is home to the Grann Kaz Plantation House, which was built in 1870, and the 'Lakaz Rosa,' a copy of a colonial servant house. The

Craft Village contains some charming, unusual goods to look at and handle.

There is an abundance of handcrafted jewelry, coconut goods, and batik apparel. The Craft Village has some very eye-catching items.

Architecture of Seychelles

Seychelles' architecture reflects its colonial background and has a distinct yet intriguing design. Lakou, kalorife, and thatched roofs were common features of traditional architecture. The roofs of the townhouses were composed of corrugated iron sheets and resembled those of the Victorian era.

Kitchens were frequently positioned outside of the residences. These historic dwellings, however, are becoming less popular and have been replaced with newly constructed residences with flat roofs, as seen in other former British colonies.

Seychelles Traditional Clothing - National Costume

The French and British colonists had a significant effect on Seychellois fashion. Kazak is a waist-length, long-sleeved shirt that was popular in the late 1800s. During the colonial era, hats and shoes were also imported from France via Mauritius.

Modern apparel, on the other hand, is made of a light cotton fabric that is ideal for the humid, tropical weather in the Seychelles.

Seychelles Religion

According to the 2010 census, Christianity is practiced by the vast majority of the people. There is, however, a lesser fraction of Muslims and Hindus.

Seychelles provides a tranquil holiday spectacular, with deep blue azure oceans washing off golden sand. The enthralling galvanization of cultures enriches and memorializes the trip experience.

Art and Handicrafts

Seychelles, a cultural melting pot with natural treasures, tells its dynamic tale through the skilled hands of its artists. In this section, we delve into the realm of Seychellois art and handicrafts, an enthralling trip that combines tradition, creativity, and the rich tapestry of island life.

Nature-Inspired Craftsmanship: Discover one-of-a-kind handicrafts inspired by the Seychelles' magnificent natural beauty. From elaborately carved coconut shell masterpieces to colorful paintings capturing the hues of the coral reefs, each work exemplifies Seychellois craftsmen's strong connection to their island environment.

Creole Elegance in Textile : Immerse yourself in the realm of Creole elegance reflected in Seychelles' vivid fabrics. Traditional weaving techniques coexist with contemporary designs to create textiles that tell the story of the islands, from the rhythmic waves to the lush tropical greenery.

Woodcarving Mastery: Seychellois woodcarvers turn natural woods into elaborate sculptures and utilitarian objects, as seen by their expertise. From the characteristic double-ended boats gracing doors to the masterfully carved furniture, each piece symbolizes the Seychellois people's cultural past and their symbiotic relationship with their lush environment.

Modern Seychellois Art Scene: Explore the modern art scene, where Seychellois artists convey their thoughts of the islands in a variety of forms. Paintings, sculptures, and mixed-media installations provide a contemporary perspective on Seychelles culture and society, as well as the ongoing interplay between tradition and innovation.

Island-Inspired Jewelry: Embrace the enchantment of the Seychelles with locally created jewelry. Each item is a wearable piece of the islands, allowing you to take a touch of Seychellois beauty wherever you go, from delicate seashell earrings to big statement pieces incorporating native flora.

The Essence of Batik: Learn about the complex art of batik, which uses wax-resistant coloring processes to bring textiles to life. Seychellois batik artists produce magnificent designs inspired by the archipelago's rich marine life, lush landscapes, and the lively culture's kaleidoscope of hues.

Coco de Mer Creations: Take a look at the one-of-a-kind handicrafts inspired by the distinctive Coco de Mer palm. The seeds of this unique and iconic tree are transformed by artisans into magnificent pieces ranging from delicately carved decorations to useful objects like bowls and spoons, offering a concrete connection to the Seychelles' natural beauty.

Seychellois Pottery Traditions: Venture into the heart of Seychellois pottery traditions, where expert potters shape the islands' rich clay into both functional and ornamental pieces. Seychellois pottery exemplifies the blend of functionality and artistry, from handcrafted dinnerware to beautiful sculptures.

Artisan Markets and Boutiques: Explore the lively ambiance of Seychelles' handmade markets and stores. Explore booths brimming with handcrafted treasures, interact with craftspeople, and learn about the tales behind each piece. These marketplaces function as creative hubs, connecting shoppers to the authenticity of Seychellois handicraft.

Art and Sustainability: Learn how Seychellois artists combine art and sustainability. Many craftsmen in the Seychelles are devoted to maintaining the natural beauty that inspires their works, from repurposed materials to eco-friendly procedures, forging a healthy link between art and the environment.

Explore the art and handicrafts of the Seychelles, where each work conveys a narrative of cultural diversity, environmental sustainability, and the everlasting link between craftsmen and their island home. Seychelles' creative landscape encourages you to explore, enjoy, and take a bit of its heartfelt creation with you, whether you're looking for a traditional souvenir or a contemporary masterpiece.

Chapter Nine
15 Reasons Why You Should Visit the Seychelles

It's a honeymoon hotspot

It's difficult to surpass the freshly remodeled Denis Island, a 25-villa resort with fantastic organic food that's already a big favorite with newlyweds.

Pristine Beaches

The Seychelles has some of the world's most beautiful and lovely beaches. The beaches in Seychelles are a paradise for anyone seeking solitude and natural beauty, from the famed Anse Source d'Argent with its gigantic granite rocks to the hidden Anse Lazio bordered by thick flora.

Features world class hotels

The Six Senses Zil Pasyon gives itself six stars, and we won't argue. The resort has massive pool villas, restaurant menus with a focus on sustainability, and convenient access via short boat trips from traffic-free La Digue. A percentage of the cost of your vacation also goes toward habitat restoration.

You can play the mogul.

Release your inner megalomaniac with a luxury helicopter trip above the islands, a fluffy white cat, a cigarette holder, and a gorgeous partner.

Marvel at the world's largest seed

The biggest seed in the world, coco de mer, comes from a kind of palm tree and may weigh up to 44lb - and the Vallée de Mai on Praslin island is the location to locate them. Wander among the whispering palms in search of enormous geckos and black parrots.

They have flying foxes

The finest free activity in the Seychelles is seeing gigantic fruit bats swooping above the bush at nightfall. If you like flying animals, go for the enigmatic Silhouette Island. The guesthouse La Belle Tortue is a hidden gem.

There is a new (affordable) spa

The Boat House restaurant on Beau Vallon Bay is a local tradition, and a day spa has been built next door. It's close to a beautiful beach and is friendly and reasonable.

There are brilliant art galleries

Who requires Gauguin? Nobody catches tropical color and light like Michael Adams, whose delightful west coast home also serves as the Seychelles' greatest art gallery. He's very shy, so ask to meet him if he's at home.

The Seychelles have an amazing views

In a positive manner, of course. The little Treasure Cove hotel in Bel Ombre conceals a terraced restaurant with one of the nicest views in the Seychelles. Ignore the cheesy LED outside sign and concentrate on the delicious Creole food and breathtaking sunsets.

The sealife is exceptional

Desroches Island in the Amirantes has been completely renovated and now provides excellent scuba diving and fishing. Book in advance to receive a 30% discount.

Beautiful coral reefs

Dive into the crystal-clear seas that encircle Seychelles to discover a thriving undersea world. The coral reefs are alive with colorful marine life, making it a snorkeling and diving paradise. Explore the UNESCO World Heritage site of Aldabra Atoll or the abundant biodiversity of Sainte Anne Marine National Park.

Luxurious Accommodations

From overwater bungalows with private plunge pools to beachfront homes surrounded by lush tropical gardens, Seychelles has it all. Seychelles offers the ideal location for a romantic holiday or a tranquil retreat, whether you want a world-class resort or a discreet boutique hotel.

Unique Flora and Fauna

The Seychelles islands are home to a range of rare and indigenous species. Visit Praslin's Valleé de Mai to see the famed Coco de Mer palm, or the Aldabra Atoll to see huge Aldabra tortoises. Seychelles is a biodiversity hotspot that provides nature enthusiasts with a unique opportunity to see unspoiled landscapes.

Island-Hopping Adventures

The Seychelles are a group of 115 islands, each with its own distinct personality. Explore the granite wonders of La Digue, the lush vistas of Mahe, and the laid-back charm of La Digue on an island-hopping vacation. Each island has its unique set of gems awaiting discovery.

Seychellois cuisine is a delectable combination of tastes inspired by African, Asian, and European culinary traditions. Fresh seafood, Creole curries, and tropical fruits are available. Seychelles provides a variety and tasty eating experience, with everything from bustling street food markets to sophisticated seaside restaurants.

Immerse yourself in the unique cultural tapestry that is Seychelles. Discover colonial architecture, colorful marketplaces, and cultural sites in Victoria, the capital city. Interact with the welcoming Seychellois people, watch traditional dance performances, and learn about the islands' history in local museums.

Appendix
Useful Resources

📍 Séchelles

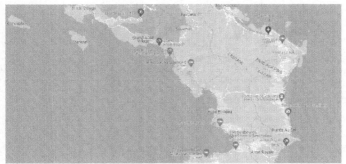

Printed in Great Britain
by Amazon